Unitarian?
What's That?

Questions and answers about a liberal religious alternative

Cliff Reed

The Lindsey Press
www.unitarian.org.uk/pages/unitarian-books

Published by the Lindsey Press
on behalf of the General Assembly of Unitarian
and Free Christian Churches
Essex Hall, 1–6 Essex Street, London WC2R 3HY, UK

© Cliff Reed 1999, 2010, 2011, 2017, 2018

First published 1999
Reprinted with revisions 2010, 2011

New edition 2018

ISBN 978-0-85319-089-9

Designed and typeset by Garth Stewart, London

Printed and bound in the United Kingdom by
Lightning Source, Milton Keynes

Contents

About the author

Cliff Reed was active in the Unitarian ministry for over thirty-five years, for most of that time in Ipswich, Suffolk, until his retirement in 2012. He was Secretary of the International Council of Unitarians and Universalists from 1995 to 1997 and President of the General Assembly of Unitarian and Free Christian Churches from 1997 to 1998.

He has written six collections of devotional material: *We Are Here* (1992), *The Way of the Pilgrim* (1995), *Celebrating the Flame* (1997), *Spirit of Time and Place* (2002), *Sacred Earth* (2010), and *Carnival of Lamps* (2015). He is also the author of *'Till The Peoples All Are One': Darwin's Unitarian Connections* (2011).

Introduction

The historic Unitarian affirmation *God is One* is what gave the movement its name. Today, this stress on divine unity is broadened. Now Unitarians also affirm: *Humanity is One, the World is One, the Interdependent Web of Life is One.* But while Unitarians may share these affirmations, we do so in an open and liberal spirit. And there is a lot more to us than that.

As a minority faith tradition, Unitarians are less well known than we deserve to be. Of those who have heard of us, many have an outdated or erroneous impression. Many more may never have heard of us at all. This is a shame. In a culture where many are once more seeking to explore life's spiritual dimension, Unitarians offer something unique.

This text is designed to introduce Unitarians by means of a simple question-and-answer formula, based mainly on questions that people have actually asked when encountering Unitarians for the first time. I hope it will begin to answer your questions.

But first, it is important to make something clear. Unitarians approach religion and spirituality in a rather unusual way. We believe that faith should be free from the constraints imposed by others. We believe that no one should dictate what another person may or may not believe. This means that this text is not the Unitarian party line, for there is no party line. It does not presume to speak for all Unitarians on any or every issue. It is essentially my own personal perspective as a lifelong Unitarian.

Cliff Reed

Who are the Unitarians?

The Unitarians are a community of people who take their religion, or their spirituality, liberally. That is to say, we hold that all people have the right to believe what their own life-experience tells them is true; what the prompting of their own conscience tells them is right. We say that each person's spiritual or intuitive experience deserves respect; that everyone's deep reflection and reasoning on religious and ethical questions should be taken seriously.

Unitarians form a movement that tries to put these affirmations into practice. Our local religious communities offer a setting where people can worship, explore, and share faith together in an atmosphere of freedom and mutual respect.

Please note: Unitarians share the first three letters of their name with some other religious groups and denominations. This sometimes causes confusion. Just to clarify matters, Unitarians have nothing whatsoever to do with the Unification Church and, with one exception, are quite distinct from any other religious organisation whose name begins with Uni.... The exception is the Universalist tradition, found mainly in the United States, which is dealt with elsewhere in this text.

Where does the word "Unitarian" come from?

Its roots lie in the Reformation of 16th-century Europe. At that time Protestant Christians claimed the right to read the Bible in their own languages and to interpret it for themselves.

Some who did so found that it spoke of one God, without qualification. This did not square with the orthodox Christian doctrine of the Trinity, which says that God consists of three "persons". Because these people believed God to be a "unity" rather than a "trinity", they became known as "Unitarians".

Does "Unitarian" have the same meaning today?

Unitarians are less likely to argue about such strictly theological issues today. We now place more stress on the importance of liberty of conscience in matters of faith.

It is still true, though, that most Unitarians affirm the oneness of God: the Divine Unity. Traditionally this was about God as one "person". Nowadays, however, God's unity is often seen rather differently: as the oneness of that Ground of Being within which we and all things come to be. Following from this, many Unitarians affirm that the infinite variety and diversity of the universe is connected and enfolded in a transcendent oneness. Thus unity is the true and essential nature of things.

Just as creation is one, so too humanity is one, and the human person is one. What divides is less important than what unites. That which unites – the ultimate unifying principle or spirit – is what many Unitarians mean today when speaking of God.

Do Unitarians have anything to do with "the New Age"?

Unitarians have been around for centuries. We are not a manifestation of the New Age movement. Nevertheless, as with any phenomenon relating to human spirituality, Unitarians are prepared to look at the vast range of New Age practices and ideas with an open mind.

Having done so, though, it must be said that many of us regard a good deal of what we see as highly suspect, even dangerous. Old superstitions have been revived, new ones developed, and populist pseudo-scholarship favoured over the real thing. We Unitarians value our heritage as rational religionists, as well as valuing life's spiritual dimension. Much New Age material seems to fail the tests of both reason and healthy spirituality.

On the other hand, Unitarians also see valid and valuable insights in some of what is dubbed "New Age". In particular, many Unitarians welcome holistic interpretations of the human person or the planet. We are prepared to see the value of some forms of alternative and complementary medicine, for example. We also share the revival of interest in a spirituality that focuses on the natural world and believes we must get back to living in harmony with it. This is an area where our civilisation has much to learn. We are also sympathetic to approaches that value the intuitive and the feminine.

The whole New Age movement reflects the spiritual hunger of our times. Some of its responses to that hunger are highly dubious, but others deserve serious, though discriminating, attention. Unitarians are willing to give that.

We would not wish to dismiss anything that genuinely meets a need. Neither, though, do we wish to retreat into the spiritual and mental obscurity of a pre-Enlightenment, pre-scientific age that is anything but "New"!

Are Unitarians Christians?

As to whether any Unitarian, or anyone else, is a Christian is really for that person to decide.

From the earliest days of the Church there have been many different ideas about what being a Christian means. Much suffering has been caused by the resultant disputes, persecutions, and wars. This sad record has led some Unitarians to regard the term "Christian" with disfavour. For them it is too hung about with unacceptable baggage to be worth retaining.

There are also those who simply do not base their belief system on the Christian tradition. Some of these define their position as religious humanist. Others favour a broader theism, an earth-centred spirituality, or a faith that draws principally on religions other than Christianity.

However, Unitarians generally hold Jesus in high regard. We favour a simple and inclusive definition of the word *Christian*. Thus a Christian is any person who seeks to live in accord with the life and teachings of Jesus, who identifies with what is best in the Christian tradition, and who, perhaps, sees in Jesus a revelation of the God who is immanent in all people. This is the wellspring of love that permeated his nature and his ministry.

In this sense, many Unitarians are Christians. And we also recognise as such all who share the same spirit, whatever their position on the Christian theological spectrum.

What do Unitarians believe about God?

"God" is a very subjective word. Unitarians recognise this and do not presume to define God for others. We believe that everyone should be free to encounter the Great Mystery for themselves "without mediator or veil", as Ralph Waldo Emerson put it.

However, most Unitarians would use the word "God" to signify that which they believe to be of supreme worth. God is that which commands ultimate reverence and allegiance. God is the inspiration and the object of those who seek truth in a spirit of humility and openness. For some, Christian language about God as a loving, personal power – father-like, as Jesus experienced – comes closest to their own belief. Increasingly, the feminine aspect of the divine is recognised too – God as Mother, the Goddess. Many experience God as a unifying and life-giving spirit: the source of all being, the universal process that comes to consciousness as love in its creatures. Some use the word "God" to signify the human ideal, the noblest visions and aspirations of humanity against which we measure ourselves. God as an inward presence – the "still small voice" –- means more to many than any external power.

Such understandings are not, of course, mutually exclusive. There are some Unitarians who avoid using the word "God" altogether. For them it has become debased or corrupted by abuse, or simply doesn't mean anything to them. Does all this sound confusing? Only if you really think that God – that which is ultimate in the universe and in our lives – can be reduced to one neat formula. Human experience suggests otherwise, and Unitarians accept this.

Do Unitarians believe in the Bible?

Unitarians see the Bible as the record of a people's long struggle to understand themselves, their world, and their God. In it the writers describe and interpret the spiritual dimension of their existence and their history. In the insights, stories, and experiences that the Bible's human authors record, we can learn much in our own quest for faith and meaning.

Where we find in scripture a source of sustaining and abiding truth, it can be said to be a source of divine wisdom. But Unitarians do not approach the Bible uncritically or without discrimination. Nor do we regard it as an inerrant and unquestionable authority. What it says must be viewed in the light of reason and conscience. Due regard must be given to the continuing discoveries of biblical criticism, serious scholarship, and archaeology.

Anything in the Bible that Unitarians accept as true is accepted because it rings true in our own humble reflection upon it. We do not accept it just because it is in the Bible. Much that is there is clearly addressed to particular cultural and historical situations. Much belongs to a remote stage of religious development to which we cannot relate.

Taking the advice of Paul the Apostle, Unitarians prefer to abide by the spirit of the Bible's sacred treasures than by a narrow adherence to the letter.

What do Unitarians believe about Jesus?

Unitarians believe that Jesus was a man, unequivocally human.

It has long been our view that to talk of him as God is unfaithful to his own understanding of himself. The New Testament accounts describe a Jewish man, chosen, raised up, adopted and anointed by God. They claim that the divine purpose was that Jesus should reconcile first the Jews and then all humanity to each other and to God. This would prepare the way for the Messianic age of peace.

Jesus stood both in the prophetic tradition of such figures as Isaiah and Hosea, and in the kingly line of David. His ministry took place in a primarily Jewish context. His challenge to a corrupt priesthood in the Jerusalem Temple made him powerful enemies. These found common cause with the ruthless Roman authorities. The result was his crucifixion, a supreme example of human integrity and faithfulness in the face of human evil. Unitarians do not see the crucifixion as a blood sacrifice for sin.

Whatever Jesus' own perception, his followers – like him, all faithful Jews – believed him to be the Messiah, "the anointed one"; in Greek, "the Christ".

Today's Unitarians are not first-century Jews. We cannot share their perspective. However, Jesus' teachings and what we know of his life lead Unitarians to regard him as a major (some would say the major) figure in humanity's spiritual journey. While honouring him, we do not worship him, something we believe he would not have wanted.

9

Do Unitarians believe in the Holy Spirit?

Unitarians do not see any differentiation between the Holy Spirit and God, and use the words more or less interchangeably. We conceive of the Spirit as the active divine presence in individuals and communities, as the divine breath that gives us life, as that ineffable factor that binds us together.

The Spirit, for many Unitarians, is the divine mystery moving among us and within us as we work and worship. Indeed, for many, God as loving, creative Spirit is the primary concept of the divine.

Do Unitarians celebrate Easter?

Most Unitarians do, but with perhaps three separate, although not mutually exclusive, perspectives.

First there is the view that in the stories of Jesus' resurrection we have a powerful myth. This celebrates the triumph of the human spirit, exemplified in Jesus, over all that would crush it, and even over death.

Second, from a more specifically Christian standpoint, is the belief that the loving spirit of Jesus triumphed over death and passed into the community of disciples who formed the early church. The body of the faithful thus became the physical resurrection, the risen body, of Christ. Inasmuch as a religious community continues to embody that loving spirit, then it continues to embody the resurrection. Most Unitarians would doubt the literal veracity of the Gospel resurrection accounts. Some, though, see them as based on vivid spiritual experiences undergone by several of Jesus' followers in the aftermath of his death. These then played an important part in convincing the disciples that his spirit was still among them.

The third principal way in which Unitarians celebrate Easter is as the festival of life's renewal in the spring. The earth's resurrection after winter's apparent death is something that affects us profoundly as dependent children of nature. Many Unitarians therefore feel that it is a time of deep spiritual significance in itself. They point out that the word "Easter" is derived from "Eastre", the name of the ancient Anglo-Saxon Goddess of spring, fertility, and renewal.

Do Unitarians celebrate Christmas?

The answer is yes. Why? It marks the birth of a religious leader of seminal importance. The birth of Jesus stands as a symbol of the divinity inherent in every human birth. It stands for the perennial rebirth of innocence and hope in every new child. It calls to mind the values of peace and goodwill that should be with us all the year. It coincides with the winter solstice, the turning of the earth towards the light and the warmth of a new year. All these factors play a part in the Unitarian Christmas.

We Unitarians do not, in the main, let it worry us that we do not know the precise date of Jesus' birth. Nor do we worry that the two quite distinct Gospel Nativity stories probably have little or no historical basis. As myth they express later beliefs about the significance of Jesus and other, more timeless, truths.

Unitarians believe that Jesus was conceived and born in the usual human manner, which in no way diminishes him – quite the contrary. Many, though, are willing, for the season, to suspend disbelief, enter into the Christmas myth, and find at its heart a message of divine love for a world that needs it.

Do Unitarians believe in the Devil and Hell?

The short answer has to be "No". Few, if any, Unitarians think of the Devil as having any objective existence. If we speak of him at all, which we rarely do, it is as a mythical being. In this sense the Devil is only the mythic personification of all the evil and malice of which human beings are capable.

The linguistic root of the word "devil" has to do with division. Therefore the Devil could be taken as a mythic symbol of that which divides what should be united – human community, the integrity of creation, the wholeness of the human person. Any suggestion that he is more than this is seen by Unitarians as a descent into superstition – with very real dangers for the psychologically vulnerable.

The same can be said for "demons" and the like. Where our ancestors, and even some today, see demon-possession, Unitarians see mental illness.

We take a similar view of Hell, traditional abode of the Devil. When Unitarians speak of Hell it is in this-worldly terms. We may use the word to describe the very real states of spiritual desolation and alienation into which human beings can fall. Hell might be described as the sense of utter separation from God, or the inability to give or receive love. Unitarians do not see Hell as the domain of an "anti-God" or as a divinely ordained place of punishment. Indeed, we do not see it as a place at all.

How do Unitarians respond to "the problem of evil"?

Unitarians tend to see the world and its inhabitants in positive terms. This doesn't mean, though, that we are not conscious of "evil". The Unitarian theologian, James Martineau, described the so-called "problem of evil" as "this old and terrible perplexity" – and so it is. Unitarians are reluctant to produce glib solutions to it.

As far as "natural evil" (disease, earthquakes, hurricanes, and so on) is concerned, Unitarians see it simply as part and parcel of living on this planet. We would not regard such phenomena as the result of supernatural agency or divine wrath. But we might want to ask just how "natural" some of these disasters really are. It is often the case that human action, or the neglect of it, can greatly exacerbate or even cause an apparently "natural" disaster. The destruction of forests, for example, is implicated in such disastrous events as flooding, landslides, climate change, and desertification. Thus the boundaries between "natural evil" and "human" or "moral" evil can become blurred.

As far as moral evil is concerned, Unitarians do not see this as an inherent or inherited feature of human nature. Let us take "evil" to describe attitudes, words, and actions that originate in malice, hatred, and ruthless self-concern. Unitarians might well see its source in a fundamentally flawed world-view, one that denies the essential connectedness of all people and all creation. However, even then we would be conscious of the immense complexity of the issue, and of our limited understanding of human motivation.

Rather than get too bogged down in theorising, most Unitarians would see tackling evil and the suffering it causes as a higher priority. As adult individuals we are responsible for ourselves. Our prime task is to examine what we do and think. Then it is to direct our own lives in such a way that they will be a blessing to those whose lives we touch.

Having done this, our responsibility extends to the wider human community. There the challenge is to respond effectively, yet lovingly, to the consequences of evil, whatever its cause.

What do Unitarians think about sin?

"Sin" is a word with baggage attached. That is why Unitarians often avoid it, or use it only sparingly. But this does not mean that we pay no attention to the issues that the word involves.

A Unitarian view of sin might be this: to sin is wilfully to act, speak, or even think in a way that one's own conscience condemns as wrong. Alternatively, sin is the failure to act, speak, or think in ways that one knows to be right. Or again, to sin is to fall short of the standards of conduct that one's own faith or ethical system regards as ideal. It is missing the mark that we set ourselves. And because we all fall short in this way, there is no room for smugness, self-satisfaction, and self-righteousness.

Although Unitarians may not like to use the word "sinners", we would agree that we are all imperfect, flawed beings when set beside our models of the ideal. However, we generally take the view that sin is essentially a personal thing. Each one of us is responsible for himself or herself, although the consequences of our sin will affect others, both now and in the future.

The remedy for sin is a process of contrition, repentance, and forgiveness. That is, true regret, a turning away from what conscience condemns, and a loving acceptance of the sinner. The giving and receiving of forgiveness – including self-forgiveness – are necessary for healing to take place. Through forgiveness (human or divine) the wholeness and fellowship that sin fractures are restored. Unitarians believe that we must always be ready to forgive. It is no part of our practice to load people with guilt. A burden of guilt is destructive both spiritually and psychologically.

The notion that we human beings inherit a burden of sin from Adam and Eve – that we are conceived in sin and born sinners – finds no favour with Unitarians. We are more likely to see the story of the Fall in the Book of Genesis as a mythical portrayal of every person's journey. It represents the life-journey from the innocence of infancy through the harsh transition of adolescence to adulthood and the awakened consciousness of sexuality, responsibility, and mortality. Unitarians see no inherent or inherited guilt or depravity here, no need for blood-sacrifice to buy back the soul. Jesus, Unitarians affirm, lived out his message of selfless love to the bitter end. Our own sin, our own false and selfish consciousness, is overcome inasmuch as we too can live lovingly and selflessly, no matter what the cost.

How do Unitarians understand salvation?

It must be said that many Unitarians are wary of the word "salvation". We find some of its associations in mainstream Christianity unhelpful.

However, whether we use the word or not, Unitarians tend to see salvation in this-worldly rather than other-worldly terms. We identify it with the deliverance of the human spirit from those things that diminish it and bar the way to its fulfilment. Thus, deliverance from all that fractures our relationships with each other, with the rest of creation, and with our own true selves – and so from God – constitutes salvation. Such fracture manifests itself in hatred and resentment, arrogance and bitterness, greed and fear, guilt and self-contempt.

Unitarians identify the agent of salvation as healing, dynamic love. This is both channelled through others and derived from some wellspring within ourselves. It is love that brings wholeness and fulfilment through the dissolution of the barriers that divide us. These barriers exist both inwardly and in the external world. The ultimate saviour is the source of love's power – which most call God.

However, love becomes manifest only in human beings and their relationships. So all those people who bring mercy and reconciliation, liberty and justice into the world are the embodiments of salvation. They are the "saviours" within humanity.

Do Unitarians believe in life after death?

Unitarians hold a wide variety of beliefs on this subject. Some have a very firm belief in personal survival beyond death, and cite evidence to support it.

Others – probably most – are less categorical, perhaps believing that in some way all that constitutes a human being continues to exist after death. However, they would not wish to be specific about how, where, or in what form. They might talk in terms of the soul or spirit returning to God. They might say that the essence of a person is rewoven into the spiritual life of the universe, just as the body's constituents are reworked into the universe's physical dimension. Some are interested in exploring the various theories of reincarnation. The persistence of a person's ideas, genes, and more intangible influences would be as much as many Unitarians would be prepared to concede. Some prefer to say nothing at all, being content to "take one world at a time". Most, though, would also point to the continued existence of individuals in the memories and lives of those who knew and loved them, and would see in this a source of comfort.

Whatever our position, most Unitarians agree that this is an area of mystery. Many theories exist, many claims are made, but undisputed evidence is hard to find. Unitarians take the view that, in any case, the focus of our attention should be this world. Our concern is better directed to considering how we should live our lives in the here and now. A life well lived is the best preparation for death, whatever may lie beyond it.

What is the Unitarian view of human nature?

Unitarians take a scientific and evolutionary view of human origins.

We regard the biblical creation stories as myths. As myths, though, they still have value. In them are expressed deep and perceptive insights into human nature and our place in world.

However, a hard and fast view of human nature is precluded by the incompleteness of our knowledge. We have a long way to go in our exploration of human origins, biology, sociology, and psychology.

Generally speaking, though, Unitarians share a positive view of human nature and human potential. While not being blind to human weakness and our capacity for evil, we do not see human beings as inherently depraved or corrupt. We have little time for the doctrines of "original sin" and inherited guilt. Rather we see human beings as having inherent and equal worth. This is regardless of all such differences as race, gender, class, creed, or sexual orientation.

Unitarians affirm that all human beings originate in the Divine Unity, all have something of God in them, all are alive with the same divine breath.

Humanity's tragedy has all too often been to lose sight of this. Thus people become alienated from each other and from the roots of their own being. To rediscover an awareness of our connectedness with each other and with our common origin is one of the objects of the spiritual quest.

On the fraught question of whether human nature and human destiny are free or determined, Unitarians come down on the side of freedom. Our forebears had little time for the old Calvinist ideas of predestination or for superstitions like astrology.

More serious considerations come into play with such issues as the influence of the environment in which we are raised and, increasingly, with genetic determinants. Although the jury is still out here, Unitarians recognise the importance of these issues. Unitarians accept that human beings are moulded by many influences and live within certain parameters. However, we believe that people remain capable of free choice and self-determination. Indeed, our freedom is enhanced the more we understand the factors that influence us. And to the extent that we are free, then to that extent we are also responsible.

Is there a Unitarian morality?

With our belief in individual religious freedom, can Unitarians give any moral guidance? If we are free to "build our own theology",[1] are we not free to build our own morality? Can there be any shared moral standards, or are all free to behave as they please?

One point a Unitarian might make is that unless your moral standards are truly your own, then they do not really constitute morality. If they are simply imposed on you, then they are just a means of social control and nothing more. Of course, a commonly accepted "moral framework" must exist in any human society. But this is not enough, unless people also have a personal morality, an ethical code that is truly their own.

A Unitarian view of morality does not favour untrammelled individualism. Unitarian acceptance of the underlying unity and connectedness of humanity comes into play here. We don't live in isolation. We are members of society, with a responsibility to help make it work. We may be individuals, with a right to our own beliefs, but we are also social beings. As such it is incumbent upon each of us to behave in ways that respect others and make our community, and our world, a better place for everyone. In building a personal morality we may well learn from the teachings and example of others, but the crucial point is to make it ours. One of the traps in the area of morality is to pay more attention to

---

1 *Building Your Own Theology* is the title of a series of adult religious education courses devised by Richard S. Gilbert, a Unitarian Universalist minister. They are widely used in Unitarian congregations.

other people's behaviour than to one's own. Judgementalism and self-righteousness can result.

Unitarians are suspicious of any morality that is too rigid in its decisions or which is lacking in mercy. Such "morality" often comes with a religious label attached. But a liberal religious Unitarian morality offers another model: one that imposes the highest standards on oneself, while treating others with justice and compassion.

Where do Unitarians stand on ...?

It is impossible to state "the Unitarian position" on any and every specific ethical and moral issue. This is for two reasons. First, there are too many to deal with in the space available here. Second, Unitarians do not impose a "moral orthodoxy" any more than a theological one.

On many things, though, there is a near-universal consensus. This may be expressed in statements agreed at local, district, and national levels. Even then the right to dissent is fully respected, and such statements are not seen as binding on all Unitarians, either in the present or the future.

Unitarians are wary of narrowly focused "morally absolute" positions – those claiming a monopoly of truth and virtue on a particular issue. We see such inflexibility as insensitive to the inevitable complexities of such issues. Simplistic "moral absolutism" also carries with it the dangers of spiritual arrogance, bigotry, and self-righteousness. It can corrupt the well-meaning. As we have seen on issues such as abortion and animal rights, it can lead to violent fanaticism on the part of extremists that discredits a whole movement.

Unitarians approaching any moral issue will seek balance and a stance that affirms love, life, compassion, and justice. We will be conscious, though, that our personal decision is ours alone. We will recognise that other sincere people may reach a different conclusion. Where there are differences, Unitarians seek respectful dialogue. Where there is consensus, we will speak and act together as the times demand.

Do Unitarians mix religion with politics?

Unitarians tend to see their faith in this-worldly terms. This means that we see the spiritual sphere as inextricably linked with the ordering of human affairs. Our religion is in constant dialogue with the world as it is, and thus with the political and social issues of the day.

In this we make no claim to be different from many people in other denominations and faith traditions. Indeed, Unitarians find many points of contact with other people of faith on matters relating to social, economic, and environmental justice.

Inasmuch as these matters are political in the broadest sense, then Unitarians do mix religion with politics. This means, for some, active involvement in campaigns, marches, and demonstrations. It may mean lobbying politicians and making legislators aware of Unitarian concerns in particular areas of policy. It means using one's democratic rights responsibly and purposefully for the common good. It means focusing on political and social issues in worship in order to explore their spiritual implications.

Unitarians are interested in the whole range of challenges facing our society and our world. We believe that our liberal religious ethos, our affirmation of human dignity, and our one-world vision have something valuable to offer in this regard.

However, although many Unitarians are active in the social and political sphere, as a movement we are not aligned with any political party or single-issue political organisation. Unitarians can be found across the whole spectrum of democratic political parties, sometimes as dedicated activists. They can also be found in all manner of groups campaigning on humanitarian and environmental issues.

As a movement, Unitarians are religious, not political, but our religion has political implications, and our politics have a spiritual foundation.

How do Unitarians view sexuality and gender identity?

Most Unitarians regard both gender and human sexuality as a spectrum and believe that everyone has the right to express their gender identity and sexuality, and to have their own understanding of these identities affirmed. These spectrums include sexual identities such as heterosexual, homosexual, bisexual, asexual, and pansexual, and gender identities such as transgender, transsexual, and non-binary. We also recognise the existence of intersex people (whose biology cannot be characterised as male or female) as part of the human sex spectrum.

Unitarians see sexuality as a natural and healthy dimension of human existence. Although it is fundamentally the means of procreation, we value its role in bringing intimacy, tenderness, and pleasure to loving relationships. We do not insist that sex is for procreative purposes only, but its primeval purpose is a source of wonder and reverence. In all sexual matters, Unitarians stress the absolute necessity of responsibility and respect. For us, sexual immorality means any form of sexual activity that is not conducted on a sure basis of mutual consent and with due regard to the health, welfare, and feelings of those involved. We regard sexual abuse and exploitation of any kind as an affront to the rights, worth, and dignity of the human person. Any sexual activity that is not entered into willingly, consciously, respectfully, and lovingly by consenting and responsible adults is seen by Unitarians as dangerous and unacceptable. In our view sex, properly used, is a wonderful gift to be thankful for. If it is squandered or used to degrade and hurt others, then something wonderful becomes tawdry and squalid.

Do Unitarians see environmental issues as religious?

As people who place their primary religious emphasis on life in this world, Unitarians are much concerned with environmental issues. Historically, we have been deeply interested both in the scientific study of our natural environment and in seeing it as a spiritual resource – alive with the divine.

This remains the case today. Unitarian devotional writing and hymnody reflect a deep sense of the sacredness of the natural world. Many Unitarians are active in environmental and conservation organisations. Unitarian worship often reflects spiritually on these subjects, and also celebrates the natural cycle of the seasons.

Among Unitarians there is considerable interest in "creation spirituality" (not to be confused with "Creationism"). Unitarians may see creation spirituality in a Judaeo-Christian context: the creation as blessing, as the pregnant manifestation of God's unfolding creative power. They may also look to other traditions which, for example, see the earth as Mother – to be revered and respected – and all natural phenomena replete with spiritual significance.

Whatever the theological underpinning (which some may not see as necessary anyway), care for the environment is now seen as an important aspect of liberal religious life. This is both for its own sake and for the sake of all present and future generations of the earth's inhabitants. Unitarians regard the maintenance of a sustainable, diverse, and beautiful environment – "natural" and "human" – as needful for our survival and our well-being as a species.

Are Unitarians pacifists?

On pacifism, as on all issues of personal conscience, each Unitarian is free to come to his or her own conclusions without fear of judgement or censure. So although there are many Unitarian pacifists, there is no explicit requirement or implicit expectation on the matter. Unitarians live with diversity and its potential tensions – on this subject as on many others. A Unitarian congregation may include both pacifists and members of the armed forces.

But whether pacifist or not, Unitarians affirm the values of peace, justice, forgiveness, and reconciliation. Some call these divine values. They are held to be necessary for the wholeness and happiness of any human community, from the family to the nation and the world.

On the subject of war, Unitarians agree that it is wrong. Some say that this rules out the use of force entirely, that it can never be justified in any situation. For others, though, there are – sadly, tragically – situations in which the use of proportionate force is necessary in order to prevent or defeat a greater evil, particularly to defend the innocent and the weak in immediate peril.

Unitarians generally agree, however, that we must find better ways than war and violence to resolve conflicts and disputes. We agree that nations and individuals should regard the renunciation of violence as a moral imperative. But many Unitarians also believe that, in the world as it is, circumstances sometimes necessitate actions for the sake of others that fall short of these ideals. It gives them no satisfaction to do so.

Where does religious authority lie?

The Unitarian view of religious authority contrasts with those held by many other traditions.

It is often the case that a religious organisation, whatever its size, vests spiritual authority in a holy book, a creed or confession of faith, in a hierarchical structure or priestly caste, or in some charismatic leader or authority figure. Although this authority may be seen by its own adherents as divine or as a mediation of the divine, the Unitarian view is that it remains essentially human, regardless of claims made by it or for it.

Unitarians are sceptical of any claim to be in exclusive possession of religious truth. In the final analysis, all human beings have the same access to the evidence. All human beings can have a direct relationship with the ultimate, with God. All human beings can see the universe for themselves. All have the potential for an interior life of the spirit.

Although someone may develop spiritually within a particular faith tradition, such development is greatest when the believer is in active and critical dialogue with it. To be unthinkingly submissive to it, on the other hand, is fraught with dangers.

Unitarians believe that the seat of religious authority lies within oneself. This is not an arrogant claim. All people develop their own belief-system, whether they articulate it or not. All people choose what to accept or reject from the propositions on offer. The Unitarian approach is, therefore, to recognise that each person is his or her own final authority in matters of faith. Our liberal religious ethos grants full individual freedom in this regard.

However, we also see the necessity of religious community, of exposure to the beliefs, doubts, and insights of others. This provides the necessary checks and balances that prevent belief descending into self-indulgence, fantasy, and a blinkered self-centredness.

To be a Unitarian is to take responsibility for one's own faith. It is to value the intuitions of oneself and others. It is to test one's beliefs against reason and conscience. It is to afford others the same right to be honest with their own inner authority as one claims for oneself.

What do Unitarians do about Religious Education?

The Unitarian approach to children's Religious Education is concerned initially with encouraging a young child's natural sense of wonder and curiosity. In this lie the roots of spiritual growth. Hearing the stories with which others have sought to make sense of a mysterious world helps them to find a language to express themselves.

Unitarians do not impose one set of answers on vulnerable minds. At every stage Unitarian RE is concerned with helping youngsters to develop beliefs that are truly their own. This involves such things as the exploration of their developing feelings and relationships. It involves learning without prejudice about their own and other people's faith traditions. It involves consideration of the various moral, ethical, and related issues that young people must face.

The aim is to provide a warm and affirming setting in which children can grow their own faith, respect themselves and others, and prepare to enter adulthood with a healthy and personal system of values.

Religious Education doesn't end there. We Unitarians believe that it should continue throughout our lives. Increasing knowledge of our own and other faith traditions is part of this. So too is gaining a better awareness of all that moulds us and our world. Unitarian adult Religious Education is, however, particularly concerned with helping people to explore, understand, and articulate their own spiritual odyssey. A supportive, non-judgemental and entirely voluntary group is the setting for this.

In such a group a high level of trust is encouraged – and pre-determined "right answers" are neither offered nor required. Adult Religious Education programmes of this kind are an important feature in the life of many Unitarian congregations.

Is there a Unitarian spirituality?

Within the Unitarian historical tradition there have been many strands. These include deeply devotional Christian and Theistic forms, as well as a strong belief in the necessity of reason.

Religious humanism has also played its part, by locating the focus of spiritual concern wholly in our life in this world, rather than in realms or beings deemed supernatural.

Another long-standing, and now resurgent, theme is that of nature or the creation as replete with spiritual significance.

In a sense, there has always been something of a shifting balance between two tendencies. On the one hand, there is the rational, scientific, and discursive. On the other, there is the intuitive, the emotional, and – in its true sense – the mystical. While there may not be a single Unitarian spirituality, it could be said that the spectrum of Unitarian spirituality covers this range.

Unitarians would not see the poles of this spectrum as in opposition. We see a healthy spirituality as one that holds in balance the intuitive and the rational. Active respect for both the mind and the deepest emotions is necessary for wholeness of spirit.

This respect for all the aspects of one's own being extends also to other people. A willingness to recognise the spiritual core of another person's faith in this profound and balanced way liberates us from the tendency to be distracted by the particular forms, concepts, and words in which they express it.

How important is worship, and what is it like?

Most Unitarians would say that worshipping together is at the heart of all that we do. Most Unitarian communities gather in their churches, meeting houses, chapels or other premises on Sundays to worship. In worship we affirm the faith and the values that we share, while being respectful of our differences.

Unitarian worship seeks to engage the whole person as well as the whole community in what goes on. Thus while the spirit and the soul are addressed, so too is the mind – the faculties of thought and reason. Even the body is included – singing is, after all, a physical activity! Sometimes the body is involved in other ways too, in movement and dance, but this is much less common.

The form that Unitarian worship takes varies considerably. There is an increasing wish to explore new forms. It is still the case, though, that most Unitarian services take a form closely akin to the hymns / prayers / readings / address format long familiar in Nonconformist churches. But while the form may be similar, the content is usually rather different, often markedly so.

The service will usually include hymns or songs. Some may be familiar from mainstream Christianity, but Unitarians have a rich and living tradition of hymn writing.

Prayer, very often of a more contemplative and meditational type, is a regular component. Both in words and in silence Unitarians focus themselves on the divine, both immanent and transcendent.

Prayer and reflection also enables the worshipper to "centre down", to draw on interior sources of inspiration and resolve.

A selection of readings is a usual feature. These may well include the Bible, but by no means always or exclusively so. Unitarian openness to many sources of insight means that readings can come from any source deemed relevant and appropriate. Thus poetry, the scriptures of other faiths, secular writings, and all manner of devotional materials may be drawn on.

There will often, but by no means always, be a sermon or address. In the Unitarian context this is a personal statement of witness by the preacher. It is offered to the listeners to use as they think appropriate. There is no suggestion that the preacher's views must be accepted. A good sermon is a sustained and intelligent discourse that reflects spiritually on an issue of either current or timeless concern.

A children's story is often told to the whole group.

A sharing of personal news may feature.

Music is a valued component of many services.

Unitarian worship often begins with a "chalice-lighting", the "Flaming Chalice" being the recognised symbol of the Unitarian faith.

Do Unitarians celebrate communion?

Some congregations celebrate Christian communion several times a year. This is a simple memorial act, associating those present with Jesus and all who have followed him. It may also look beyond the Christian tradition to embrace all people of goodwill, whatever their faith. Unitarians also celebrate other forms of communion, notably the Flower Communion. Devised by Czech Unitarian minister Norbert Čapek in the 1920s, this is a celebration of unity in diversity, both within the congregation and in the wider world.

The various forms of Unitarian communion, traditional and otherwise, are concerned with the celebration of connectedness, sharing, and community. They express in a simple and informal ritual the links we have with each other in the present and with those in the past in whose footsteps we follow. They may also express our membership of the wider humanity and the whole matrix of life on earth.

All forms of Unitarian communion are open unconditionally to anyone who wishes to participate in the spirit of goodwill.

Do Unitarians carry out baptism?

The short answer is "yes", but short answers can be inadequate. It is necessary to stress that Unitarians differ from mainstream Christian doctrine on this.

Unitarians believe that human beings are essentially pure and innocent when they are born into the world. That is to say, we believe that a newborn child is free from any burden of inherited guilt or "original sin". No Unitarian would say that Christian baptism is necessary in order to save the soul from purgatory, hell, or damnation.

Because of such unfortunate associations, many Unitarians do not use the word "baptism" at all. Unitarian infant or child baptism is actually a ceremony of thanksgiving and celebration for a new life.

It is also a time when the parents, godparents, families, and friends dedicate themselves to the child's nurture and upbringing. The ceremony also welcomes the child into the religious fellowship, the "Universal Church", and the wider community of humanity and of life on earth. It does not have to take a Christian form.

Adult baptism is unusual among Unitarians. It takes place when an individual wishes to make public witness of her or his commitment to Christian discipleship and the way of Jesus. With adult baptism, as with the welcoming and dedication of a child, Unitarians plan the ceremony with maximum input from those most centrally involved. In this way every effort is made to ensure that it is a true and honest reflection of what they believe.

What are Unitarian weddings like?

No two Unitarian weddings are exactly alike. This is because no two couples getting married have precisely the same beliefs and aspirations about what they are doing. Unitarians help those planning their wedding to make it an occasion that is unique to them.

If the ceremony is really to mean something, then it is essential that it reflects what the couple really feel. In preparing for the wedding, the couple are encouraged to talk and think very seriously about what they want for the ceremony and, more importantly, for their continuing life together.

Rather than impose a standard form on weddings, Unitarians help couples to plan their own service. This includes not only choosing favourite readings, hymns, and music but (more importantly) choosing and even writing their own vows. Nothing is imposed that the couple do not want or cannot say in all sincerity (provided that certain legal requirements are met). Unitarians believe that for a couple to plan their own wedding service is the best preparation for it. The minister, or celebrant, is ready with advice and guidance only.

Unitarians impose few preconditions on a couple, other than that they be truly and seriously committed to their relationship as life-partners. The fact that one or both of them may have gone through a divorce is not, in itself, an obstacle. Unitarians think that people should have the chance to build anew, and to do so with the blessing of the religious community.

Unitarians are also happy to marry couples where the partners are of different faiths, and to reflect both faiths in the service.

Same-sex marriage

The Unitarian General Assembly gave its support to the introduction of same-sex marriage in England and Wales and Scotland in 2012, building upon its support for inclusion and equality for LGBTQ+ people. Each individual congregation has to register its building (if it has one) and either appoint authorised persons or ensure that a registrar is present in order to undertake a legally valid same-sex marriage. Unitarian congregations are often the only churches in a local area to have done so.

Conversion ceremonies from civil partnership to same-sex marriage may also be held in registered premises. A few Churches are registered to perform civil partnerships in religious premises. Blessing ceremonies continue to be held after a civil ceremony.

Further information is available on the General Assembly website at www.unitarian.org.uk and in person from the appropriate local congregation.

What do Unitarians do about funerals?

Wherever possible a Unitarian ceremony to mark someone's death – and to celebrate his or her life – should be true to that person and sensitive to the needs and feelings of the bereaved.

Even if the minister or celebrant did not know the deceased personally, she or he will make every effort to make the funeral service reflective of that person's qualities and beliefs. Consultation with relatives and friends is usually a part of this.

It is also an opportunity to offer pastoral care if needed and requested. We Unitarians do not use the emotional vulnerability of those in mourning to "evangelise" or impose our own beliefs on them.

Respect for the deceased's convictions is very important, and Unitarians are usually willing to provide celebrants for those who might otherwise find it hard to find one, such as humanists.

Unitarians propound no particular view on whether the dead should be buried or cremated.

Do Unitarians have ministers?

A trained and educated professional ministry has always been an integral component of the Unitarian movement, and this remains the case.

In the Unitarian context, the minister is not a member of a distinct priesthood. There is nothing a minister does that, in principle, a lay person may not do. A minister is simply a person who has been prepared and appointed to fulfil a role that others may not have the time, the inclination, or the skills to fulfil themselves. A minister is a leader of worship, a pastor, an educator, a counsellor, a facilitator, and perhaps the representative of the faith community in the wider society.

Appointment of a minister is in the hands of the congregation, not the denomination, although the denomination keeps a roll of ministers as a way of maintaining personal and professional standards.

The Unitarian ministry is open equally to women and to men, and has been so since the early 20th century. It is open to homosexual and to heterosexual people – with no prejudicial conditions imposed on either.

The Unitarian movement also has lay people fulfilling a ministerial role in some of its congregations. Such recognised lay leaders must undergo appropriate training. Sometimes lay leadership is a preliminary step towards gaining full ministerial status.

The General Assembly Interview Panel ensures that appropriate education and training opportunities are provided for those seeking to become Unitarian ministers; it currently works in cooperation with colleges in Manchester and Oxford, and with other educational bodies, including providers of distance learning. A flexible approach is increasingly being adopted to meet individual needs.

How do Unitarians get on with other churches?

Unitarians have always had a somewhat ambivalent relationship with what are called "mainstream" Christian churches. The ambivalence can come from both sides. Both historical theological differences and recent trends influence the relationship.

However, Unitarians have generally sought as close and constructive a relationship with other denominations as both are comfortable with. In the nineteenth century a leading Unitarian[2] proposed, in vain, the formation of a "Federal Union of Churches". Unitarians were active in the foundation of the British Council of Churches, but we have so far been excluded from its successor, Churches Together in Britain and Ireland. In local situations, Unitarians have often been closely involved with ecumenical activities. Sometimes, though, we have been excluded here too, and sometimes we have not wished to be involved.

Unitarians have no desire to indulge in theological disputes with the Christian mainstream. We are content to respect the faith and beliefs found in other churches, even if we do not share them. However, Unitarians and mainstream Christians have a great deal in common too, both historically and spiritually. This is particularly so when it comes to putting shared values into practice. In all sorts of areas concerned with social responsibility, pastoral care, global justice, environmental issues, and human welfare, Unitarians can and do find common cause with mainstream Christians.

---

2   *The Life and Letters of James Martineau*, James Drummond & C.B. Upton, 1902.

What do Unitarians think of other faiths?

Human beings are infinitely varied. So too are their cultures and the conditions in which these evolved. Furthermore, the universe and its mysteries – including the human psyche – cannot be entirely comprehended by our limited powers of thought and description. For these reasons Unitarians recognise the inevitability of many diverse expressions of faith.

Unitarians do not say that all religions are the same. Nor do we say that all are of equal worth. What we do say is that no honest and sincere expression of belief should be discounted out of hand. To judge another's faith is presumptuous and dangerous. All true expressions of the religious impulse come from our encounter with the wonder and mystery of the universe. All result from the joy and pain, the highs and lows of our life-experiences in this world. Thus all have something to say and to teach.

However, between the original experiences at the root of a faith tradition and the development of its religious institutions much can happen. Interpretation, rationalisation, elaboration, and corruption come into play. At every stage what happens is subject to the vagaries of human beings. This means that any claim to absolute and exclusive truth must be treated with the utmost reservation, if not suspicion.

Thus Unitarians afford respect to all sincere believers of whatever faith. We seek to learn from the witness of all spiritual traditions, but we do not do so uncritically.

Unitarians were pioneers in the area of interfaith dialogue, and founded the world's oldest global interfaith organisation, the International Association for Religious Freedom. Unitarians are also active in many local interfaith organisations and initiatives.

Who founded the Unitarian movement?

Unitarians do not look to any one person as the founder of the whole faith tradition. Many people played their part in the emergence from mainstream Christianity of a liberal religious movement with a Unitarian theology. In fact, Unitarian ideas have developed independently several times in a number of places around the world.

The oldest Unitarian movement in the world with a continuous history is in Transylvania – now part of Romania. Unitarians there look to Francis David (1520–1579) as the founder of their Church.

Another early figure of great importance was Fausto Sozzini (1539–1604) (better known to history as Faustus Socinus). He was an Italian theologian who became the effective leader of the Unitarian Minor Reformed Church of Poland, also called the Polish Brethren.

In England several names are worthy of special mention. John Biddle (1615–1662), a young schoolteacher, publicly propounded a Unitarian theology during the religious and political ferment of the mid-17th century. Joseph Priestley (1733–1804), best remembered as a scientist, became the leading spokesman for the Unitarian movement of his day, which grew within the English Presbyterian and other Nonconformist denominations during the 18th century.

Theophilus Lindsey (1723–1808) left the Church of England to found the first avowedly Unitarian congregation in Britain (in Essex Street, London) in 1774.

The Unitarian movement had its pioneers elsewhere in Britain too. During the 18th and early 19th centuries they included such figures as Jenkin Jones and Charles Lloyd in Wales, and William Christie and Thomas Fyshe Palmer in Scotland.

Although the social conventions of the time kept women out of leadership positions, this did not stop them from contributing to the developing life and thought of the emergent Unitarian movement. Sadly, their names were often neglected by historians. Among them, though, were the pioneer feminist Mary Wollstonecraft (1759–1797) and the poet and educationalist Anna Laetitia Barbauld (1743–1825).

What does the Flaming Chalice mean?

The Flaming Chalice has become the generally accepted "badge" of Unitarianism over the past fifty years. It was first adopted by the American Unitarian Service Committee during the Second World War. Since then, Unitarians throughout the world have seen it as a way to express their distinct identity as a liberal religious community.

The man who designed it was a Czech named Hans Deutsch, and his inspiration was the Czech religious reformer, Jan Hus. Hus was burned at the stake in 1415 for the "heresy" of offering the chalice of communion to the laity as well as the clergy.

Recalling this, we Unitarians offer our own "chalice of communion", symbolising the religious community itself, to all people without condition or reservation. When and where Unitarians actually celebrate communion, the understanding becomes literal as well.

The flame atop the Unitarian chalice represents the spirit of love, truth, and liberty. To this spirit the community bears witness and with it, hopefully, the community is filled. For some, at least, this recalls the "tongues of fire" of Pentecost.

The flame also has a more tragic significance. It commemorates the martyrdom, not only of Jan Hus, but of so many who died bravely in the cause of religious liberty.

What holds the Unitarian movement together?

Unitarians believe that freedom from prescribed creeds, dogmas, and confessions of faith is necessary if people are to seek and find truth for themselves. We rate spiritual honesty above religious conformity. But without a binding creed, how can a congregation – let alone a national movement – stay together?

The Unitarian answer is that shared values and a shared religious approach are a surer basis for unity than theological propositions. Because no human being and no human institution can have a monopoly on truth, it is safer to admit that from the outset. We are seekers and sharers, fellow pilgrims on the path, and this is how we Unitarians see ourselves. The values underpinning the Unitarian movement have to do with mutual caring and mutual respect. They involve a readiness to extend to each other a positive, involved, and constructive tolerance. They are the values of a liberal religious community that honours individuality without idolising it; of a community that finds spiritual stimulation in the unique contribution of each person while feeling itself united by a bond too deep for words. They are the values of a community that is open to truth from many sources; a community of the spirit that cherishes reason and acknowledges honest doubt; a community where the only theological test is that required by one's own conscience.

Above all, perhaps, Unitarians are bound by a sense of common humanity. We believe that the world would be a better place if more people put this one factor before all the lesser and illusory things that divide us.

How is the Unitarian movement organised?

The basic unit of the Unitarian movement is the autonomous local congregation. It may be called a church, a fellowship, a chapel, or a meeting. There are about 180 of these in Britain. They vary in size, but membership is usually in the tens rather than the hundreds. Some have their own buildings, while others hire space for their activities, or meet in private homes. Distribution across the country is very uneven. These congregations associate together for the purposes of mutual support and shared endeavour. Thus at both the regional (district association) and national levels they comprise an interdependent federation or denomination. The structure is democratic at every level.

The national organisation is called the General Assembly of Unitarian and Free Christian Churches. This has departments and committees dealing with such things as ministry, religious education, youth, social responsibility, worship, information, development, interfaith matters, and finance. There is a department dealing with Welsh affairs: a high proportion of the twenty-one congregations in Wales use the Welsh language.

The General Assembly also owns and administers the Nightingale Centre, a conference, retreat, and holiday centre in the heart of the Peak District National Park at Great Hucklow in Derbyshire.

Unitarians who are unable to reach a church or fellowship are catered for by the National Unitarian Fellowship with postal/internet contact and some regional meetings.

Within the Unitarian movement there are a number of organisations catering for specific constituencies and interests. These include women's groups and young adult groups, societies interested in Unitarian history, church music, and psychical studies, and open fellowships concerned with peace issues and with meditation.

The General Assembly has a close association with the Non-Subscribing Presbyterian Church of Ireland. This shares the same freedom from imposed creeds and dogmas but is overwhelmingly liberal Christian in theology. As a denomination, it does not identify itself as Unitarian, although it includes people who do.

Are there Unitarians in other countries?

There are Unitarian and Unitarian Universalist groups in at least twenty-five countries on six continents. Some are relatively large and long-established, others are very small and very new.

Most are members – along with Britain's General Assembly – of the International Council of Unitarians and Universalists (ICUU), which was established in 1995. Each member group is independent, with its own history and traditions, and they vary considerably in both theological emphasis and cultural setting. All are committed to a liberal approach to faith.

The largest is the Unitarian Universalist Association, in the USA. This is also the most pluralistic in theological terms. Second largest is the Unitarian Church of Transylvania (in Romania), which is wholly Christian in its Unitarian faith.

The ICUU fosters understanding and closer relations between its member groups, organising activities and events for this purpose. These range from courses for strengthening leadership in small and newly emerging groups around the world, to theological conferences and symposia – the proceedings of which are published.

To be a part of a congregation in any one country is also to be a part of the global fellowship fostered by the ICUU.

Who are the Universalists?

The Universalist tradition dates back at least to the 18th century. It began by preaching universal salvation as opposed to the predestined consignment to heaven or hell propounded especially by orthodox Calvinism. Universalists held that God's love would not permit anyone to be damned eternally, and that everyone could and would be saved eventually. This Universalism evolved to a position that saw universal truth reflected in all the great faith traditions.

In Britain the few Universalist congregations that existed in the 18th and 19th centuries soon became part of the growing Unitarian movement.

In the United States, the Universalist Church and the Unitarians grew closer and closer together until, in 1961, they merged to form the Unitarian Universalist Association. Some of the newer movements around the world have taken the double Unitarian Universalist name from the outset.

Unitarians and Universalists, while having their own historical and theological traditions, now form one integrated faith community.

What sort of people become Unitarians?

· People looking for an open-minded religious community whose individual members are free to develop their own truly personal faith.

· People looking for a liberal church where they will be free to voice doubts – where they are not expected to say things that they don't really believe.

· People looking for worship that engages the mind as well as the spirit and the emotions.

· People who want a universal religious approach, open to the insights of more than one faith tradition.

· People who want a spiritual foundation for their humanist values and their social and environmental concerns.

· People who want a church that engages seriously with the Christian heritage but is not bound by it.

· People in search of something to give balance and depth to their awakening spirituality.

· People in search of a welcoming and undogmatic religious community for themselves and their families – however defined.

· People who take humanity's spiritual dimension seriously but want to move beyond fundamentalism, sectarianism, and religious intolerance.

Where can I find out more?

Unitarian Headquarters will be happy to deal with your enquiries or put you in touch with your nearest Unitarian congregation. They can be contacted at:

Unitarian Head Office
Essex Hall, 1-6 Essex Street
London, WC2R 3HY, UK

Tel: 0207 240 2384
email: info@unitarian.org.uk
web: www.unitarian.org.uk

Further reading

Living with Integrity: Unitarian Values and Beliefs in Practice
edited by Kate Whyman (Lindsey Press, 2016)

The Unitarian Life, edited by Stephen Lingwood
(Lindsey Press, 2008)

The Larger View: Unitarians and World Religions,
by Vernon Marshall (Lindsey Press, 2007)

On the Side of Liberty: A Unitarian Historical Miscellany
by Alan Ruston (Lindsey Press, 2016)

These publications are available from the address on the
previous page.

Index